THE PROPHET AND THE WITCH

John Kennedy Brown

authorHOUSE

AuthorHouse™
1663 Liberty Drive
Bloomington, IN 47403
www.authorhouse.com
Phone: 833-262-8899

Published by AuthorHouse 01/10/2025

ISBN: 979-8-8230-4125-6 (sc)
ISBN: 979-8-8230-4124-9 (e)

Library of Congress Control Number: 2024927679

Print information available on the last page.

This book is printed on acid-free paper.

CONTENTS

SUPERSTITION

Let's establish a few things, I grew up around people that was very superstitious and dealt in witchcraft. Now to them, that was more real than the Word of God. I want to share this also, to whom we yield our minds or bodies to; we become servants too. Romans 6:16 says, Do you not know, that to whom you present yourselves to obey, you are his slaves to obey; whether of sin leading to death, or of obedience leading to righteousness. Listen, whatever we learn as children becomes a part of our lives. When things aren't challenged they remain the same.

Webster defines witchcraft as: (a) the use of sorcery or

magic (b) communication with the devil or a familiar (c) rituals and practices that incorporate belief in magic and that are associated especially with neopagan traditions and religions.

Lets look at superstition Webster defines it as: (a) a belief or practice resulting from fear of the unknown, trust in magic or chance or a false conception of causation. My grandmother kept superstitious sayings in our ears almost every day. Here are some that was taught to us: (1) If you break a mirror, that's seven years of bad luck; To which there were Two remedies: (a) Throw a piece of the broken mirror in running water; or (b) bury the mirror face down. (2) Don't take the trash out at night, because it's bad luck. (3) Don't dropped peanuts shells on the floor, guess what it's bad luck. (4) If a black cat cross your path to the left, it's bad luck; they say crossing your fingers will keep you safe. (5) If you step on the back of someone's heel, hit them hard three times in the back to prevent bad luck. (6) If you step on a crack you break you mother back. (7) If you spill salt, that's bad luck. (8)Walking under a latter, is bad luck. (9) If you point your finger at a funeral home or hearse, your finger will rot off; unless you bite your finger so hard that you leave a teeth print on it. (10) When a bird peck on your window, it's bad luck. (11) If you're walking with someone and you split a pole, you will be separated. (12) If your left eye jumps, that's bad luck. (13) If your hand itch, you will be receiving some money. (14) When your nose itch, someone wants to see you. (15) Carrying a rabbit's foot with you, suppose to bring you good luck (not so good for the rabbit). (16) Putting a horse shoe over your door, suppose to bring you good luck. (17) If you spill wine, someone will die. Note this, someone is going to die; whether you spill wine or not. Hebrews 9:27 says, And as it is appointed for men to die once, but after this the judgment. Generally, on New Years Day many people will cook a traditional meal to bring them good luck; it consists of cabbage greens, corn bread, black eye peas and ham hocks. Now we know that all menus are not the same, because we're dealing with different races; but some are similar. There's nothing wrong with these foods, it's the thoughts and beliefs that's been programmed into the minds of the people; because if you prepare them for me any time during the year, I'm going to eat and enjoy them. Personally, I can do without the black eyes peas, perhaps macaroni and cheese will fit me better.

Are all traditions wrong? No, only if they oppose the Word of God. Mark 7:13 says, Making the word of God of no effect through your tradition, which you have handed down and many such things you do. Webster defines tradition as: the handing down of beliefs and customs from one generation to another. Many things I was told by people turned out not to be true. But, if you told me that I would have been angry with you. One reason is this, my grandmother is my flesh and blood; surely she wouldn't tell me anything wrong Second, we don't want those that we have confidence in to be wrong. It could be a relative, friend, pastor or associate; when it comes to ministry, we don't want our leaders to be wrong. Brother Brown, have you been wrong before when it comes to teaching the Word of God? Yes I have, not only about spiritual matters; but natural things too. When it comes to the Gospel of Yeshua or (Jesus) He is not a denomination. The gospel of Jesus Christ is the heart of Yahweh (God) reaching out to all humanity. The Father, the creator of the universe is a Spirit and they that worship Him; must worship Him in Spirit and in truth. John 4:24

One guy told me that his denomination was the only one teaching the truth of God almighty. Sadly, he is not the only person that feel this way about their denomination. I then shared the Word of God with him, but it was quickly rejected. Mark 9:38 says, Now John answered Him saying, Teacher we saw someone who does not follow us casting out demons in your name and we forbade him; because he does not follow us. (39) But Jesus said, do not forbid him; for no one who works a miracle in My name can soon afterward speak evil of me. (40) For he who is not against us, is on our part. That guy told me these scriptures was irrelevant, because they were wrote in so and so AD.

All the scriptures was wrote in a certain time era. He was taught by his denomination what to say, when someone ask certain questions. It can be dangerous for me or anyone else to preach the gospel from our denomination. Why? Because if I am self-righteous I preach a baptist gospel. A church of God in Christ gospel a pentecostal gospel. A four square gospel or an assembly gospel or what have. The gospel is for all who receive it. The bible doesn't teach that there is a white, brown, yellow, red, or black gospel. The gospel of Jesus Christ goes beyond color barriers and reaches the hearts of people. It's good to have a personal relationship with Yahweh. Some individuals want their pastors, leaders and others to do all their studying, reading, meditating praying and fasting. It's not given for my pastor to become a (god) in my life. Psalm 42:1-2 As the deer pants for the water brooks. 2. My soul thirsts for God, for the living God. When shall I come and appear before God. When you know and stand on the Word of you shouldn't be moved by every wind and doctrine that comes along. The word of God is right but if you hear someone say something about the Word of God. If you are not sure about it, take it as second information until you see it for yourself Acts 17:11 These were more fair- minded than those in Thes-sa-la-ni-ca in that they received the Word with readiness, and searched the Scriptures daily to find out rather these things were so. There was one minister that didn't allow his members to bring their bible to service. He told them that he would tell them what they need to know. Another leader threw his bible to the floor and told his members to listen to him. Another person threw their bible to the floor and I said I am beyond this. I am filled with the Spirit.

We shouldn't throw our bibles away. The bible holds the Word and Spirit of God. So how can anyone get beyond the Word of God. The Word of God and the Spirit they agree. God will never fight against himself. This is what Jesus said, John 10:30 I and My Father are one. A pastor told me that a minister said to him if you find the people dumb leave them that way. 2 Timothy 2:15 Study to shew thyself approved unto God a workmen that needeth not to be ashamed, rightly dividing the word of truth.

Over the years I've found out that tradition doesn't allow us to think only to react. Not all man made traditions are bad but there are some that oppose the Word of God. Yahweh All mighty traditions are correct. 2 Thessalonians 2:15 So then, brothers, stand firm and hold to the traditions that you were taught by us, either by our spoken word or by our letter. COLOSSIANS 2:8 See to it that no one takes you captive by philosophy and empty deceit, according to human tradition, according to the elemental spirits of the world, and not according to Christ. Matthew 15:3 He answered them, And why do you break the commandment of God for the sake of your tradition. 1Corinthians 11:2 Now I commend you because you remember me in everything and maintain the traditions even as I delivered them to you. Matthew 15:6 He need not honor his father. So for the sake of your tradition you have made void the Word of God. Secret sororities what about them? Man have always established a brotherhood because he knows how important unity and fellowship is. That can't be argued because there is strength in numbers. There are some sororities that are of God and are very beneficial to many people. There are some sororities that are open in Jesus name but are not of Him. Just because something is private doesn't mean it is bad all the time. Matthew 5:15 Nor do they light a lamp and put it under a basket, but on a lamp stand and it gives light to all who are in the house. When joining a group, club, or any organization it is always good to be prayerful about it. And see how God will lead you. It's good to find out things about the organization you wish to join. Even if you are seeking to join a ministry put Yahweh first and stay prayerful. He will speak to you about that matter and everything that matter to you. Jeremiah 33:3 Call to me, and I will answer you, and show you great and mighty things, which you do not know. God is speaking even when He is quiet. One minister said you can go off as much as what God doesn't say as what He does say at times. White magic the beautiful side of evil which is a lie. When have you known the devil to have a beautiful side. Isaiah 5:20 Woe to those who call evil good, and good evil Who put darkness for light, and light for darkness, who put bitter for sweet and sweet for bitter. A diamond back rattle snake is beautiful but don't to get close to it because it is dangerous. White magic by many is consider to be harmless or innocent but how can the devil or evil become good. White magic is said to be a protection remedy against evil spirits and forces. Can Satan kingdom be divided? Luke 11:18 Jesus if Satan also be divided against himself, how shall his kingdom stand? Because ye say I cast out demons by Beelzebub. White magic has traditionally referred to the use of supernatural powers of magic for selfless purposes. White magic deals five elements air, Spirit, earth, fire and water. Now these sources can be innocent in nature. But once a person faith and wrong motive is placed with these things they give it life. I was praying with a group of people one night. Yahweh showed me this young lady hands I told her be careful how you lay your hands on people. When I said that her mother gave her a strange look and said I told you about putting your hands on people like that. Is touching people wrong? No but if your motives isn't right pure there is an evil attach to it and some folks know how to do the devil bidding.

The Spirit of Yahweh gave me a vision concerning a witch that had turned an hourglass upside down toward me. Yahweh didn't allow one grain of sand to fall. Psalm 33:10 The Lord bringeth the counsel of heathen to nought and maketh the devices of the people of none effect. An evangelist told me that a pastor control his congregation with a cup of water. Years later I got acquainted with brother Sal he and I enjoyed talking about God. Every day our conversation basically was about Him. Brother Sal shared with me how spiritual his mom is he said I want you to meet her. I agreed and was elated that I would be meeting Mrs. Stable. When I met her I discovered she was very knowledgeable about the Word and Spirit of God. Just about every day I would go to Mrs. Stables house my cousin saw me one day. Len said you better stop going over Mrs. Stables house she is going to get you. When he told me this I immediately rejected that statement because he was known as a clown he loved to horse play and wrestle you even if you didn't feel like it. He was the boy that cried wolf when he told me about Mrs. Stables he had a smile on his face so I said Len isn't serious at all. Here's what I wasn't expecting to hear from the Spirit of God. As he is sharing that statement with me I actually felt the anointing of God in me confirming what Len was telling me about Mrs. Stables was correct. But I overrode what the Spirit of Yahweh was saying. At times God speak things to us about people that are close at times, we don't want to hear it. So what can we do about it nothing but receive it and act accordingly. I remember being over Mrs. Stables house one day with five people. We join hands to pray while she is talking I heard a sweet calm voice of the Holy Spirit said she is lying. Without thinking I quickly said to her I heard a voice said that you are lying. Here's her cover up lets rebuke that devil later I found out that was the Spirit of Yahweh warning me about her. Think before you speak my mentor told me he was in a church earlier that day talking with a lady evangelist in a vision a witch flew in on a broom.

He said to himself ok God am I talking to the witch or is someone coming in later?

It's not always good to blurt out everything that God is telling you. We must have the wisdom of God in our lives. I was sharing with a person just because God speak to you about a person. Doesn't always mean that He wants you to share it with them. This person became angry with me and said I don't care what no one says. If God shows me something about someone I am going to tell them. We were in the front yard praying one day Yahweh gave me a vision about this person. I went to tell her when I did He said be quiet. She's not going to hear what is being said so I kept quiet. A couple days later while talking to this person God had dealt with her about what He told me to be quiet about. I could have disobeyed God and prove an empty point to myself. Now if God have told or tell you to share messages with people find yourself doing so. Isaiah 58:1 Cry aloud, spare not, Lift up your voice like a trumpet:

Tell my people their transgression, And the house of Jacob their sins. Jeremiah 31:3 The Lord has appeared of old to me, saying: Yes, I have loved you with an everlasting love.

Yahweh wants us to clearly share the gospel of Jesus with a firmness and boldness. At the same we are doing this let's not forget to display our love walk with people. So cry loud and love His people. John13:35 By this shall all men know that ye are my disciples, if ye have love one to another. If a transfer truck is coming up the high way going eighty-miles per hour. Your son is one year old sitting in the middle of the street I doubt it very seriously you would whisper. Andy sweetheart mommy need for you to come back in the yard. You would probably yelled to the top of your voice. ANDY SWEETHEART THERE IS A TRUCK COMING GET OUT OF THE ROAD!!!!! There would be frowns in your face not so much that you are angry but concern for the safety of Andy. Some people when they preach they feel the anger of God concerning the people sins. It's not for us to go around thinking that we are judge, jury and prosecutor because Jesus Christ is the righteous Judge. 2 Timothy 4:8 Finally, there is laid up for me the crown of righteousness, which the Lord, the righteous Judge; will give to me on that Day and not to me only but also to all who have loved His appearing. We all need to learn to how to judge and examine ourselves. There was a person they were self righteous and anointed. He felt like he was right about everything. This person went around sowing discord and confusion and we shouldn't do that as christian. We know that people are going to die because it is an appointment that we all have. Hebrew 9:27 Yahweh told me that he didn't die because of what he did but because of what he refused to do. That was to repent! Some people feel like it is no need for them to repent. Some say that they don't do or say anything wrong so why should I repent. Lets see what the bible says Acts 3:19 Repent ye therefore, and be converted, that your sins may be blotted out, when the times of refreshing shall come from the presence of the Lord. Every born again believer should find himself repenting. Acts 17:30 And the times of this ignorance God winked at; but now commandeth all men everywhere to repent.

Earlier I was sharing with you my relationship with Mrs. Stables. I had place a great deal of confidence in her perhaps too much. When she called herself giving me a word of knowledge by the Holy Spirit she was off. I wanted it to be from God because she was speaking. She once told me God Almighty called her to be the mediator between heaven for all humanity. At first I wanted to believe her but I was disturbed in my spirit. Once again she was lying let's see who the mediator actually is the only mediator. 1 Timothy 2:5 For there is one God and one mediator between God and men, the man Christ Jesus. At times Yahweh is telling us things and we don't get it or understand specifically why He is saying that. At any time Yahweh can speak to us with a clarity and there will be no, if and nor but about it. What God was showed me about Mrs. Stables we were driving on the Mississippi bridge when God showed me an ape jumping up and down. Concerning her at that moment I had no idea why He reveal that to me. I was happy to share that story with brother Sal. He said my mother told me that she be bother with an ape type spirit trying to attack her. Actually it was deeper than that, that was his cover up. She had that spirit in her. I began to notice somethings I had blinders on. She would control her children and talked harsh to them and cussed at them. She would be very up sat with them that ape spirit would manifest. Mrs. Stables told me God wanted to tell me something. She instructed me to get a cup of water and place it under my bed. I didn't know any better so I followed her instruction. She was using that cup of water to control me I started feeling strange for no reason. I told my cousin what Mrs. Stables had told me to do he looked surprise and didn't give me a comment. Weeks later when we were talking he said, do you remember when I asked you to go get me something out of the store? I said yes, he said I didn't want anything but when you left the room I removed the cup from under the bed and threw it away. I found out Mrs. Stables was practicing witchcraft that's when I separated from her and her son. The Spirit of God told me that someone had buried a picture of me. I'm thinking why in the world someone would bury a picture of me. I later discovered that when that picture fades away my life suppose to fade away with it. That have been over forty years ago. I thank Yahweh for His protection. He's real and truly there is none like Him. Psalm 33:10 Yahweh bringeth the counsel of the heathen to nothing and maketh the devices of the people of none effect. One woman of God shared with me that a couple had buried some bones on me and the Spirit of Yahweh started fighting against them. Until they had to dig up those bones because nothing was going right for them. There was a man that was growing sicker as each day passed by no one knew what was the problem. This woman told another woman you need to take that stuff off that man. She went in the yard and dug up a can of lye she had buried on him. She waited too late about the time she dug it up he had died. The crossroads while in my twenties I met a musician he and his wife was blind. They were very friendly and showed me a great deal of hospitality whenever I visited them. They called him (son) he and I were conversing one day. At that time I was clueless about what he told me. He said they tell me that you can go to the crossroads and ask for anything that you desire. That sound interesting to me because who don't want to receive everything they desire. Son didn't tell me the whole story I had no idea that the crossroads is of the devil. Mark 8:36-37 For what shall it profit a man, if he gain the whole world, and lose his own soul. Or what shall a man give in exchange for his own soul. You will never receive anything from the devil without him getting something from you. Many individuals have gone to a crossroad and gave their soul to devil for success. Some have been famous and none famous man is triune he consist of three parts. 1 Thessalonians 5:23 And the very God of peace sanctify you wholly; and I pray God your whole spirit and soul and body be preserved blameless unto the coming of our Lord Jesus. Man body one day will die but the spirit and soul shall continue to live in an eternal place. There is a heaven and hell and one will be able to miss both of them.

A warlock was invited to a television show to help the cast perform witchcraft they wanted a more realistic atmosphere. He said something that need to be noted he said these people are actors and actress. But witchcraft don't know that you are acting or pretending. People use witchcraft for different reasons. Witchcraft is the casting of spells and the performances of magical rituals. There was a warlock and an evangelist that ended up in the same city the warlock went to the evangelist and this place is not big enough for the both of us. At the end of the day the warlock was dead. Their was a christian family and a witch family the Christian family had a son. The witch family had a daughter the son and daughter began dating the young woman she was attractive. We know that there is nothing wrong with beauty and being handsome. At times people play their looks to their advantage. His family warn him to stay from her but he refuse to do so. One night he became intimate with her and shortly after that he died. This woman told me as a child she and other would have seances trying to talk to the dead. She said they called for her dead dog to show up. One day they were talking to the devil, she said a dog started barking. Now what's happening is a familiar spirit has manifest. Familiar spirits are evil spirits that pretends to be a dead relative, friend or a living person or animals. Leviticus 9:31 Do not turn to mediums or necromancers; do not seek them out, and so make yourselves unclean by them: I am the Lord your

God. Isaiah 8:19 And when they say unto you, inquire of the mediums and the necromancers who chirp and mutter should not a people inquire of their God? Should they inquire of the dead on the behalf of the living. Lets see what Ecclesiastes says about the living and the dead. Ecclesiastes 9:5-6 For the living know that they shall die but the dead know not any thing, neither have they any more a reward; for the memory of them is forgotten. Also their love, and their hatred, and their envy is now perished; have they any more a portion for ever in any thing that is done under the sun. Their was a woman who practice witchcraft that went to the grave yard. Then dug up this young guy body and ask it did my son kill you. The body responded and said yes but lets keep it real. It wasn't that person it was an evil spirit speaking. Lets remember what Ecclesiastes 9:5-6 says many people think they are conversing with their dead relatives, friend or associates. I have been around people when the wind blew the screen door open. They would say come in so and so speaking of their dead relative. But the decease don't know any thing hear nor see anything. So people are being deceived by these spirits. I think every one wants to hear from or see a relative that has passed on. One reason why people go to mediums and psychic is an attempt to do so. Medium is the practice of purportedly meditating communication between spirits of the dead and living human being. Psychic Webster is person who claims to speak with or for the dead. Some psychic and medium do have the ability to reveal truth to you. One reason that many have familiar spirits Webster familiar spirit is a spirit or demons that serves or prompts an individual. Those spirits are familiar with family lineage or ties. When you deal with psychics or mediums they have the ability to yield to these spirits. Thus receiving an answer from them. These spirits were with our fore parents and they came down to different generations. It's not strange for that (go between) psychic, medium to tell you that your grandfather ate vanilla ice cream and cookies each Saturday morning. They have knowledge of our family history but they are not like Yahweh all knowing. Familiar is the Latin word familiars, meaning a "household servant," and is intended to express the idea that sorcerers had spirits as their ready to obey their commands. Those attempting to contact the dead, even to this day, usually have some sort of spirit guide who communicates with them. One day a woman shared a story with us. She said her daughter sent her a doll that she purchased from a rummage sale. At first she said something would pull the blanket from her while in bed. When she looked she saw no one after several more incidents she finally saw it was the doll. She said she got the doll and tied it up in placed it in her in junk house. The next time she looked outside in the junk house it was untied. She said she burned the doll up. You don't know when you buy things from garage sales what spirits are attached to them. Neither when you buy some new items also.

One of my prayer partner called me one night to pray with this lady she knows. She explained to me that things in her house were moving on their own. After that I prayed in faith with her believing that God had already worked things out for her. The next day I spoke to her over the phone I ask her how things were. When I said that she said with a surprise the bible just moved. I asked her what did she think was going on. She said I purchase some crystals in brought them in here. A light went off in my head I said that's the problem get those crystals out of your home. There was another couple that put a ceiling fan up in their home. The husband and wife started lusting after other people after searching for an answer it came they discovered. That the ceiling fan that was made in china had a symbol on it. It was a picture of Lady Godiva. She would ride on her horse through the streets bare back while her hair would covered some of her body. The husband and wife got rid of the ceiling fan when that happen their relationship returned to normal. Sister Sims told me her cousin wanted to borrow twenty thousand dollars from her. She said she refused to do so her cousin told her you will give me twenty thousand dollars one way or another. She said her cousin went to graveyard with some sticks and started walking back and forth while chanting. After that Sister Sims said she got sick and had to be hospitalize. When she got out her bill was twenty thousand dollars to the penny. Trying to play both sides of the fence we were outside under the carport. At that moment something was wrong with my back, this evangelist prayed for me and I felt the presence of God. She was truly anointed by God Almighty and had spiritual gifts operating in her life. She said something that disturb me she said if I wanted to I can give a person a paper bag with flour and it and get money from them. Because I already know what is going to happen in their situation. Some people have true gifts from Yahweh but choose to play games with people lives along with their gimmicks. I was talking with a person one day she said you know you can do this and something will happen. I told her that wasn't God her reply well, all I know is that it works. Some individuals don't care if they get assistance from Yahweh or the devil. As long as they receive something it doesn't matter. There are many people that are desperate and impatience in life until they don't to wait on Yahweh. I want what I want and I want it now I have been guilty of this hundreds of times in my life. I have heard many great men and women of God preach and teach on faith through out the years and it has always been a blessing to me. I also thank Yahweh for sharing with me through his Word that faith has a partner and it is patience. Hebrews 6:12 That ye be not slothful, but followers of them who through faith and patience inherit the promises. Everything we pray for or desire want always manifest the same day, week, month or year. Many things that God spoke to me personally and through others for my life didn't manifest until around twenty some years later. If you asked me did I enjoyed the waiting I will be honest with you (NO!) There was times I got angry with God and people because I thought He wasn't blessing me quick enough. Yahweh always have our best interest at heart even when we don't realize He does. I had to pray and get in a place with the Father because staying angry and frustrated wasn't helping me any. Dirt for sale a man started selling dirt out of his back yard. It suppose to have been bless dirt to help you in life. One of my mentors told me there was a person that had a shop. It was open in (Jesus name) but the activities were not of God. There are lots of people that are saying this and that about Jesus Christ. It helps us as believers in Jesus Christ to know what the bible says for ourselves. So when people say things about the Word of God we want eat up everything they tell us. I was riding with my cousin one day I told him that people don't mind strengthen the devil's hands and his people. By given accolades and their finances to them.

But when It comes to God folks there is a problem with some blessing them. I also told him individuals pay good money to purchase colored water from these witches and warlocks. A couple of more times I repeated myself without knowing why. That's when he pull his car onside the road and stopped. He said get out I want to show you something we walked to his trunk he unlocked it. Guest what was in it colored water. I told him that I don't know what you are trying to do but you need to find a man of woman of God to pray for you. I said lets pray he was in agreement we did.

THE PROPHET AND THE WITCH

The Prophet and the Witch this young prophet was invited to speak at a church service. When he made it there the peoples were in worship. The first person he notice was a beautiful woman in a blue dress with long black hair if Michael Angelo had recently sculpture. She also had a glowing smile that commanded attention from others. He began thinking perhaps this my wife and I hope that she is single. After service he introduce himself to her it went well they began talking and soon started dating about three weeks later he started going over her house having prayer service. An instruction from Yahweh to the young prophet but not heeded. One evening he was over her house having pray service at the end of the meeting she walked in the back room. While in there the Spirit of Yahweh spoke to the young prophet in a vision by showing him a stop sign which meant stop in this relationship don't take it any farther. Minutes later she comes from the back crying he asked her what is wrong she replied He told me not to take this relationship any farther. Both received an answer the young prophet had made up his mind about her he wanted her to be his wife. Both continue in this relationship I notice at times its not that we don't hear from God. Its because God is not saying what we want to hear. There have been time when Yahweh have spoke to me and I didn't like what He had to say. I couldn't do anything about it I have tried to convince Him what He really was trying to say. All the while the truth remain What He told me is what He said, by me rewording the Word didn't change what He meant. Young prophet Johnny and sister Kim relationship seemingly grew stronger and stronger as each hour passed by. He began to talk to her about marriage she was in agreement with him. Sister Kim took him to see her family the meeting went well with the mother but her children was distance and chilly toward him they were all grown. Several months after visiting the family the young prophet notice Sister Kim mother had a negative mentality when it came to relationship. Here's what it is if you catch a fool bump his head. Many people that have that mentality also will tell you to have a spare tire. You never know when you will need it. Does the apple fall far from the tree? Sister Kim shared with Prophet Johnny a few times that her mother and aunt would go to witches and warlock for things to get better in their lives. She also told him that she went to a warlock when her son got in trouble. She wanted him to cast a spell so he would get out of jail and trouble. I remember my mother telling me a guy she knew, told her that he went to a (two head) person. He wanted this person to put a spell on him so every one would like him. My mother said that everyone didn't like Jesus so everyone wasn't going to like him. A woman ask me to pray with her concerning her fiancé. While we were praying Yahweh showed me a two head snake in the Spirit. A two head snake is known as a two head person an individual that practice witchcraft. When I told her about the vision she didn't like that she gave me a bewilder look. Years later as we talked she ask me do you remember you told me you saw a two head snake? I replied yes she told me that was her husband he was using witchcraft on me and he was having our biological daughter. Many times instructions or warnings comes to us about peoples and things and we choose to ignore it I have been one of those person. The end results never turn out in our favor. Farther warnings for Prophet Johnny concerning Sister Kim. One day Prophet Erick was conversing with Prophet Johnny he was told Prophet Johnny she smells good and looks good but she can't go with you. Prophet Johnny knew exactly why that statement was made. It was the Spirit of Yahweh speaking to him through Prophet Erick. The young prophet wanted to see what this seasoned minister had to say about his relationship with Sister Kim. Thou the answer was already given. Bishop Kenneth didn't give him an answer he said you give God a three day fast and see what He tells you. I had a decision to make years ago I ask one of the brothers what would you do in a situation like this. He responded its not what I would do but what you would do in your situation. One night Prophet Johnny was outside near Sister Kim mother house this elderly man walked up to him and said why are you out to night? You must be ready to get into some devilment the prophet said I am out enjoying the night air. The elderly man said I have been living here all my life I know everybody here. He talked for three minutes and said young man I been living here all my life I know everybody here. The elderly man kept talking the next five minutes he says for the second time then a third time I have been living here all my life. Prophet Johnny began thinking what is he trying to tell me. At that moment a car drove up behind this elderly man before he got in he gave me a smile and said young man don't take any wooden nickle.

What comes to my mind is a reminder to be careful in one's dealing. The next time Prophet Johnny talked to the elderly man he asked him what he meant about don't take any wooden nickles. He slowly and confidently said their are people that pretend that they really love you and that they are into you but they are not. Prophet Johnny knew exactly what the elderly man was telling him it was about Sister Kim. Sister Kim been told Prophet Johnny it was her way or the highway. Prophet Johnny over heard Sister Kim mother said this about him don't worry about him because he's not going anywhere. Sister Kim also told Prophet that he wasn't on her level. Prophet was telling Sister Kim baby sister that the reason your boyfriend is angry with you is that he wants to be around his other lady. Sister Kim holler out and said Prophet Johnny that's the way I feel about you. Prophet Johnny looked at her strange. Then she started laughing and said I was joking. There are somethings in a relationship that a man or woman should never joke about and that's one of them. However there are people that are immature and don't take life serious nor value relationships as they should. Sister Kim was using magic trying to control Prophet Johnny the longer they stayed around each other the bitter the relationship became. How can a witch and prophet or a prophetess and a warlock lovingly get along. 2 Corinthians 6:14-15 Don't be unequally yoked together with unbelievers. For what fellowship has righteousness with lawlessness? And what accord has Christ with Be-li-al? Amos 3:3 How can two walk together unless they are agreed. Agreement is a power tool it brings harmony and soundness to situations. Prophet Johnny was talking to Evangelist Shirley and from no where if you will. Evangelist said you are going to be minding your own business. And you are going to forget all about her around two weeks later. Prophet Johnny lost interest in her and stop his fellowship with her. For a little while she had tried to make contact with him but prophet said he didn't want to get entangle in her web. I once heard Dad Grace said a smart spider always prays before he leaves the house so he want get entangle in someone else web. Luke 18:1 lets us know that men are always to pray and not faint. Sometime we look at the enemy as being far off from us or we know people that don't like us. So we watch and pay attention to them. But what about the ones that are right under us we sometime over look. Because we are comfortable with them. We have a relationship with them and we can only see the good. And we always over look the bad or should we? The bible teaches us to know them that labor among us. And we beseech you, brethren, to know them which labor among you, and over you in the Lord.

Printed in the United States
by Baker & Taylor Publisher Services